"The highest form of knowledge is empathy, for it requires us to suspend our egos and live in another's world."
Plato

"A person often meets his destiny on the road he took to avoid it."
Jean de La Fontaine

CONTENTS

CONNOR ALLEN

DOMINOES

LUCENT DREAMING

First edition

Dominoes
Published by Lucent Dreaming Ltd.
103 Bute Street, Cardiff, CF10 5AD

Cover illustration by Kamila Krol.

ISBN 9-781-7396609-1-8

Lucent Dreaming acknowledges the financial support of
Books Council of Wales and Creative Wales.

CYNGOR LLYFRAU CYMRU
BOOKS COUNCIL of WALES

To PEJ

You were the first superhero to me.

*You are and always have been
the colour in my grey.*

Love you always

X

DOMINOES

I

DOMINOES

HAMMOND DRIVE

Hammond Drive just off Cromwell Road
Is where my story first got told
Acting bigger than big and dreaming bold
Our ambitions were like currency but never sold
Houses were cold
Mums couldn't afford gas or electric
So you'd chuck on another hoody or a blanket

Days were spent in the big car park
Group of friends and a football
With the patches torn off at our feet
Motorbikes revving up and down the street
No fathers around so all we had was each other
Just us and our single mothers

There were no locked doors in Hammond Drive
In and out of each other's houses we went
Days spent
Playing up and acting tough
Childhood dreams drawn out with chalk on concrete
Dreaming of, acting out, what we could potentially be

Jaffa having a fire in his back yard
While wannabe gangsters rolled around
Trying to act all hard
On odd days we'd take ourselves to Kemp Park
Surrounded by basketball hoops, goalposts, fields of grass

We were more than an estate
We were a family
My mum would always invite everyone round for tea
A community
Wanting to break free
Of the bullshit stereotypes and adverse poverty
It moulded me into who I'd grow up to be
It moulded us
The characters
Of Hammond Drive

That much I now see

See, Hammond Drive is where I grew up
The place everyone said was so rough
The estate was what made me so tough
But the estate was also full of so much love

A lot of shit went down in Hammond Drive
The estate it made me strive
Made me dream
Of a better life

There was never a dull moment
Fighting in the street and screaming in the neighbour's face
Was all normalised in this place
We'd have front row seats to the drama that would be
kicking off
Like we were all living in a modern day Chekhov
Making more of your life than the stereotypes was a must

Drug dealers, gangsters were some of the first
superheroes to us
Had more chance of being like them than we did of being
legit
Getting a good education, a well-paid job and shit
Making more than the £50 a week on the dole
Or falling into a depressive hole
Where you contemplate selling your soul
That black magic shit
Single mums are in their kitchens
Tightening the band, injecting their latest hit
It's sad because they won't quit

Kids not understanding the impact it could have on
your life
Carrying a knife for protection
Not scared to add another soul to their collection
Too young to process the consequences
Too young to even care
It wasn't fair
Cards were already dealt
Absences always felt
Others were beaten by belts

I always had a dream it would be different
I always had a vision I was gifted
That I wouldn't be another statistic
I would soar past all the bullshit

All around the port people love to bitch and moan

But Hammond Drive is more than an estate
See Hammond Drive is my home.

DOMINOES

TALES OF A LIGHT-SKINNED YOUT

No way u fingerd her up Beechwood Park
Bruv ur havin a laf
Sunz out
Bare people out
Wit dem kids on swingz
U want us 2 believe u fingerd
A propa rude ting like Amy

I fingered her.

Lafs from all da boys echo out
No doubt James chattin shit
As usual.
Go on then recount wot happend?
Cos we all knw wit out a doubt
U ain't fingerd a rude ting like Amy

I'm tellin you. I fingered her.

Roll out ridin round
On BMXs wit da stunt pegs on da front
1 ridin 1 balancin on da handle barz
Searchin wide n far
We out on da hunt
Lookin for dem boys 2 confront
Dem boys who jumped Toffee

Armour of a tracksuit carried us in2 war
Sumtimes
It brought Feds at da front door knockin
Stashin wot we cud in da boards of da floor
Hoppin over da back wall
Taught neva 2 b a grass
See dem blue lights, legs run so fast

Pull up by BlackAsh Park
Stealf mode its startin 2 get dark
Invisible
We approach dey hav no clue
Sneak attack but
Wot r dey guna do?
Numbrz speak volumz
Wen its 4 against 1
Crack 2 da jaw
Stamp on da floor

An we dun.

THE END OF A LAMBRINI BOTTLE

Carnival rolls around
Just once a year
Pill's poppin'
Booties dropping
Communities floating
Down Commercial Road
One cup in your hand
Housing Rum & Coke
A likkle bit of lime
The sound system
Booming out Beenie Man
Everyone falls in love
Sometime

Smells of jerk mixed with Magnum bottles
Would lurk in the ether of the field
Tempers would fray back in the day
From a look, an action, or something you'd say
To a stranger you don't know
A stranger passing by
Someone dirty looking you
You'd sneak them on the sly

All up in their face
Two loudmouth girls get rowdy
Looking to erase the other
Circle surrounds them like a Beyblade arena

Claws are out like Selina Kyle
They're pulling on each other's hair
Screaming obscenities
Punches upon punches for a while

Hooded Grim Reaper barges through the crowd
Hiding death up his sleeve
Hoping to relieve his sister of battle scars
Quicker than anyone would believe the bottle
Is revealed
Chunky: unopened
Full

A thud echoes out
Loud and deep
The white of a skull.

Body on the ground
Silence fills the crowd
Not a whisper, not a sound.
Grim Reaper exits as quick as he enters
Damage done
His sister won the fight
The other on the ground
Eyes rolled back
Fighting for her life

RUBBERS

Growing up it was just me and my brother
If you didn't want us, why didn't you wear a rubber?
Snooping around with different women undercover
Leaving all the responsibility to our mother
To raise us into the men we are
The men we've become
Because you weren't around
And yeah that was sound
To just leave us
Not give a fuss
About the lives you had a hand in making
I bet you're still out there co-creating
With numerous different baby mothers
So do the world a favour and use some fucking rubbers.

DOMINOES

THE BRANCHES OF ME

Another Black life gone
As the world just watched on
From the screens of their camera phone
A Black man lay face down on the concrete, all alone.
A Black life screamed *I can't breathe*
Another screamed for his mum
As time began to freeze
One neck under a knee
Squeezing all potential possibilities and future opportunities
What do those moments mean for me?

I mean look at me,
Really LOOK at me

When you rest those eyes upon me
What do you see?
Do you see my complexion?
Do you see my ethnicity?
Do you see the generations of my family tree
Who have faced adversity and slavery?
People chanting the word monkey?
Like crisp brown leaves blowing in an autumn breeze
Their narrative, their culture is written in the ripples
of the seven seas.
Do you see the history that has come before me?
The history that makes up our genetic key
The salty sands of Jamaica all the way to rainy Wales

My story of colour is made from the finer details.
It's in the traditional Jamaican dish of ackee and saltfish
It's in the lush greenery and landscape of Wales
Where if all else fails, a cwtsh prevails.

It's Home.
It's Love.
It's me.

Even though my complexion is the first thing you see
My complexion doesn't define me
It's just made up of the intertwined branches of my family tree
See I'm going insane, walking around with all this pain
Having to explain my heritage over and over again

Black has different shades to it
Black has different layers to it
Black has a unique history behind it
Black is part of my inner conflict
But I will not quit, I will not submit
Not until the world commits
To seeing the beauty Black has in it
The beauty every shade brings to it

WHAT DO YOU SEE?

When people look at me Black isn't always what they see
All they see is my light skin
But fuck it, I'm in this game to win.
From Jamaica to Newport
I got the best of both worlds
Black and white
If you wanna disagree then let's throw down and fight
Because I'm done with all the negativity. It's toxic.
As is all the corporate ticking of boxes.
I've heard your microaggressions for years
Amplified over the past couple of months
Coming outta the mouths of just bare ignorant cunts
On Twitter, Facebook, all of the socials.
Got so many members of my family and community feeling emotional
Feeling angered, feeling vexed.
The other day my cousin sent me this text:
Yo, cuz
How're you?
Sorry we ain't spoke in a while
But with another Black life gone
The comments I was seeing were just vile.
A video of it. Like murder porn on someone's phone
That just hits me in my feels with a darker tone.
George Floyd there all alone.
The words that haunt and stick are I can't breathe
They're more than just words because the issue interweaves

Into our psyche, into our being, our past, our present
Our Kings and Queens looking down from the heavens
I just feel like I can't do this anymore
This whole us and them narrative
It is like we're at war.
It's exhausting
It's frustrating
I read the other day in the UK
There's more Black lives in prison than in university.
That hit me real deep you see.
Like when Chadwick left his imprint on our community.
I just want the next generation of Black and mixed-race girls and boys
To make some constructive noise
Imagine the best possible world
When they're playing with their toys.

I feel you, cuz, I really do
You know I'm here for you when you're feeling low
It'll get better in time
We have to believe that we're here for a reason
And that may be to extinguish these demons

That text really got me thinking
Really got me feeling
That so many of us need time for healing
Time to amplify our dreaming.
I'm not pretending
That I want to blend in -
I want society to be more accepting.
What I'm saying is common sense

I'm not scared of causing offence:
If Black is a tall, thick, beautiful tree
And so many of the intertwined branches are what make
me, me,
Let me just ask you something
Look beyond what you initially see
Look and embrace a community
Of Black and mixed-race Kings and Queens
Who just want to be seen
Who just want to be heard
Who just want an equal and justified place in this bold
new world.

COLOURLESS

So, my mum is white
My dad is Black
Let's just dismantle that

They say the blacker the berry the sweeter the juice
Was that really the case when ancestors were
hanging from a noose?
Like livestock shackled in chains they couldn't cut loose
Being raped by slave owners in order to reproduce.
I can deduce that was in order to create
The next generation of slaves.
The legacy of generational trauma
Of abandonment.
Now it's plain to see
The trauma cages me
The constant struggle with this relationship to my past
Is robbing me of my present.

But what does it mean to be grey?

GREY

I wish I could ask my father
What does it mean to be grey?
To think everyday you're different
Confused by the mixture of DNA

Made to feel you don't belong
Even though you want to stay
Even though you were born here
Everything seems to drive you away

Grandad bled for this country
My family fought in two world wars
But Dad didn't feel he could hang around
With the echoes of their monkey calls

My fear of abandonment
Dad's fear of staying the same
These are the ghosts that chase us
The legacies of our name

They didn't need Willie Lynch's letter
To break my ancestors before me
They won't need to pound my flesh now
When ghosts haunt my family tree

My past robs me of my present
A gift from oppressor to oppressed
It's cyclical, it's inherited
From one to the other to the next

The breakdown of the Black family
It's traced from plantation to present day
The breakdown of the Black man
Who broke and ran away

My father was told he was nothing
So that's what he became
Became an echo of an absence
A reflection of that grey

SOUL

Afros are known as soul hair
But why does my soul feel so bare?
When it comes to me I know he doesn't care
But I still search for answers
Man, that ain't fair

I still seek acceptance
But no one there to confirm it
I reached out for love
It wasn't there
I reach out for comfort
It wasn't there
I reach out for you
And you were never there
29 years
Still so bare

I WONDER...

...if tears are just the words
Our mouths can't speak?

ll

LOVE

Love is bargaining with time and space
That together, in this place,
While I look upon your face
See your body all in lace
Kiss your lips, get a taste
Hold you in this passionate embrace
We explore this emotional database

Love is accepting all my insecurities
The ones that fester deep down inside
Following me around, weighing me down
Like a Grim Reaper of old
They say a problem shared is a problem halved
And sharing my problems with you
Is the best thing that I can do

Love isn't one big thing
It's a million little things
It's not about the size of a ring
Or the diamonds that make the bling
It's about what's deep down inside
What's bubbling within
It's not like it is in the movies
Love is hard
Love can make you mad
On its best days Love can make you sad
But the one thing that Love can most definitely do
Is make you better and heal you

YOU

What is it about you and your face,
Every smile, every crinkle, every trace
That I just can't seem to erase.
When I'm alone with my thoughts
I feel lost in space
Just thinking about you.

SANDCASTLES

In case I'm not here tomorrow
Let me beg, steal, borrow
A moment of your time
To let you know what's on my mind
Simply ask you *Why?*

If I breathe in 1, 2 and 3
Would you finally understand
That I crave you and me?
If I told you all my secrets
Would you promise not to leave?
Build a sandcastle with me
To harbour my vulnerability.

In another lifetime
The parallels of you and me
Would see a sandcastle withstand the test of time
So, I'd wait a whole lifetime just for you.
Just for us.
I wish I was good enough for your heart
Wish I could drop the *Why*
And be good enough for our heart.

Will you miss me when I'm gone?
Does that make me a somebody
Or am I still simply just
No one?

THE STORY OF BRIDGET

Bridget had been accustomed to monsters,
In some form, all her life.
Ever since she was a little girl
Monsters seemed to occupy her world.

She couldn't escape them,
No matter what she seemed to do.
So she carried all that fear,
Released it through her tears
That she cried.
The tears:
They filled both her eyes.

Until
One day she met a new monster
Carrying Rage on both shoulders,
Red mist surrounding this new figure.
But her heart
It grew bigger
And bigger.
The more she came to understand him
Her eyes knew different,
Saw him how no one had seen him before.
Opened up her heart,
Loved him
That little bit more.
She weakened him with a kiss,

Cared for his soul -
Saved him.
From himself.
Showed him what Love is,
Showed him what Love was.

I SEE

I see

Your perfect wedding dress
On a Cardiff side street
For all to see
Perched in a window
In all its magical glory
Long sleeves staring at me
I wonder have I lost the best thing to ever happen to me

I see

Faded images of your dad walking you down the aisle
Like worn out photos at the bottom of a shoe box
Edges torn
Colour drained
Loved ones sitting observing the show with a smile
But the one at the altar isn't me
It's someone else

I see

Your hand clasped in their hand
A smile raised from point to point on your face
And I'm sat asking myself
Am I gone from your thoughts?
Because in all of our time together
You never had that smile on your face
Am I now erased forever?

LIKE BEFORE

Hold me like you've never held anyone before

Look at me like you've never looked at anyone before

Love me like you've never loved anyone before

And I'm yours

LETTER TO YOU

Dear You,

You say I don't care.
Quite frankly I don't think that's fair
Because I can't bear the thought
Of you thinking I don't care
Because I do -
That much is true.
Care about you.
I know I may not show it
As well as I should
But that's on me
For constantly feeling guilty:
All those thoughts and feelings that you don't see
Because they're buried deep down inside of me.
But c'mon that's me down to a tee.
I know you'll agree
That I'm not as open and free
As you'd like me to be.

Look, I gotta get this off my chest
Because you're nothing like the rest
You take me at my worst and at my best
So why the hell would I think of you any less?
If anything I think of you more
That's the part of you I adore
The part that makes my heart rate soar

The part that's caring, reassuring and so much more.

When I look into your eyes all I want is you.
That feeling is nothing new -
I've felt it from the first day I laid my eyes on you
You probably don't have a clue.
It sounds silly to say I want every single part of you.

I want your lips on my lips
My hands on your hips.
I want to hear you laugh
It makes me feel warm.
I want you to feel excitement, joy, and so much more.
Everything that you deserve.
I want to run my hands all over your curves
Look into your eyes as I observe
But please accept my apologies if I occasionally swerve
The odd question that comes my way
I just don't know what to verbally say.

It's because I don't have the answers
I don't know what to do.
But one thing I do know
I unconditionally love you.

HERE WITH YOU

I don't want to let go
I don't want to give up
I want to believe I won't find anyone
Better
I don't want to close my eyes
I don't want to wake up
I want to stay here with you
Forever

NAN

Sleep now
Sleep well

There's a number in my phone book
That won't ever ring again
I take a moment
Count from 1 to 10
Then it hits me
I won't ever see you again

I'm in a tram
Riding around Amsterdam
It's just me
Working out how to be free
From this mental instability
Soul-searching
On my lonesome without friends or fam
Because you're gone.
My nan

The question of mortality
Got me lonely in this reality
No more glory
No more you
No more lessons
No more story

The memories
They follow me
On the tram tracks of the city
Carrying me
Forward
To the sandy shores of time

Good or bad. Happy or sad. Long, short, detailed
Or brief.
Memories are what we keep.
What we remember.
So their stories, and their life, live on.

HEART & MIND

My heart and mind has been under attack
So I've been away for a bit but now I'm back
I'm not gunna lie
Lately I ain't been feeling myself
Struggling with the accumulation of newfound wealth
Character assassinations and mental health

Did I go insane?
Trying to figure out how to navigate my trauma and pain
Expecting a different outcome
Reliving it over and over and over again
Am I on the right path or on the wrong road?
To be honest lately I don't even know

When I look in the mirror I see myself looking back at me
I know the apple didn't fall that far from the tree
There's cracks of my father staring back at me
His mannerisms, his charm
His way with women down to a tee

With all the cards that were dealt
Sometimes I wanna run away from myself
And never look back
Because I almost broke
When my heart and mind was under attack

I WONDER...

...if the shattered glass of a broken heart
Can ever be fixed?

DOMINOES

DOMINOES

STILL AWAKE

Why am I still awake at 3 in the morning?
I mean I'm not even yawning
I'm not tired but my brain is constantly wired
With a thousand and one different thoughts
I'm sitting in my own head
With a fishing rod
Waiting for a thought to get caught
So I can reel it up and focus on one

No matter how hard I try
Thoughts just keep swimming on by
So, awake I remain

But every so often a thought will catch
And on to it I'll latch
Try to focus on what it is
So I can try to detach

I'm scared of dying
I know that's quite a common thought among people
The thought is quite rational
But it's not fashionable for a man to be feeling that way
Well, not in this day
That's the conflict of
Do I let that thought stay
Or do I let it disappear?
Or do I let others hear what I have to say?

But just like that the thought's gone.
I'm still awake
Thinking to myself for fuck sake
But another thought latches on and I reel it up

I'm scared of becoming like my dad
That thought alone makes me mad
It's the one thing growing up I wish I had
That alone, it makes me sad
Feeling sad for something I never had
Then I feel bad for getting mad
Because I'm scared of becoming like my dad

That thought's gone away
I'm back to fishing inside my own brain
Thoughts just passing by
I'm overthinking
Laying in bed not even blinking
Chadwick in my head and a quote I read where he once said

> *Purpose is an essential element of you. It is the reason you are on the
> planet at this particular time in history. Your very existence is wrapped
> up in the things you're here to fulfil.*

That quote kills. Gets me in my feels
Because the burden can be heavy
The path I'm on can at times be lonely
I can't always be scarface, Tony
What is my purpose? I don't know
I guess all I can do is continue to grow
Continue to learn

Hopefully the burden won't burn
I can give back to others in return
But wait -

That thought's gone
And another one latches on

It's about where I've come from
Wanting to give back to my mum
Who's sacrificed everything
To make me the man I've become

This pressure I put on myself
To achieve success and not digress into a complete mess
At 3 in the morning it's getting me stressed
I have to confess
All I want for her is the best
So I put it on myself
To provide that for her before she's laid to rest
But that thought's gone as quick as I've worked out
where it's from

I try so hard to stay in my own unique lane
But this pain
Is giving me nothing to gain
The thoughts whizzing inside my head are making me insane
It's not the frame of mind I want to be in
I just want to discard all these thoughts into the
metaphorical bin

Because all my life I've been running and running
Never standing still
Wanting to keep busy before the thoughts in my head
start to make me ill
But the thoughts they keep spawning and spawning

And that's why I'm awake at 3 in the morning

TIRED

im so tired of breathing
im so tired of the trauma i carry from my dad leaving
im so tired of looking up to the stars and grieving
im so tired of being hopeful and not having something to
believe in

im.
just.
tired.

SYMPHONY OVERLOAD

Each thought is a record
Playing on repeat
Like a symphony
All at once at the same time
Thousands of records playing
And playing
Noise
Sound
Fighting to be heard
Battling to be listened to
I'm trying to focus
Figure out which is which
What am I listening
Or trying to listen to?
Focus on one
So all I hear is one
Song
Filling the space
Filling my head
Can't shut off the noise
Can't focus on one
All I hear is sound
Noise
Playing on repeat
Like a record, all at the same time

SOMETIMES

Sometimes I forget to breathe because I'm in a world of my own.

Sometimes I walk down the road and think about complete shit with no relevance.

Sometimes I'm not in the zone.

Sometimes I'm fiery and passionate.

Sometimes I overthink.

Sometimes I'm forgetful.

Sometimes I wanna apologise to my mum for all the shit I done.

Sometimes I sit alone with my thoughts.
Racing through my head. Trying to burst out. But still I sit.

Sometimes I just stand still as the whole world passes me by.

Sometimes I'm indestructible.

Sometimes salt runs down the cheek of my face.
As unspoken words fill my eyelids.

Sometimes I wonder if my irregular heartbeat is down
to the fact it's been stitched back together so many times.
Like there's more thread than muscle in my chest.

Sometimes, shut the fuck up, read the room.

Sometimes I think should I change my name to Why.

Sometimes I want to live in a Polaroid, like I'm suspended
in time.
In that particular flash of a moment.
Forever.

Sometimes I love you.

Sometimes I'm fragile.

Sometimes I'm sat on the edge of a cliff looking down
at a sea of floating thoughts and infinite possibilities.

Sometimes I'm alive.

Sometimes I wish it was me taken, not you.

Sometimes Rage and Bitterness flows through the
roadmap of my body.
It's a familiar friend.

Sometimes I remember I'm human.

Sometimes I hate you.

Sometimes I think I could burst with the amount of love I have to give.

Sometimes I think *Why me?*
What have I got to offer this scene artistically?
Like, why me?
Why me particularly?
I ain't doubting my ability or even doubting my credibility
If I have any
I don't know
I'm just saying, *Why me?*

Sometimes I ponder on hate being such a strong word that a carefulness needs to be asserted when using it.
But still, I hate you.

Sometimes I stand still and the Rage of my past lays its hand on my shoulder.
He's caught up with me.

Sometimes.

Just.

Sometimes.

PUNISHMENT

I've got bravado
But I'm a sensitive soul
There used to be Rage
That filled this absent hole

I know all of your flaws
You know all of mine
You were the one that said to me
Just give it time

See
Love isn't a twisted game
So yeah, I'll take some blame
Got busy chasing fortune and fame
But now
There's a pain that resides
Deep down inside
Tears I try to hide
When memories and accusations
Glide through my mind

Some days ok
Some days a mess
Some days my heart is put to the test
Of its limitations
Of how much it can take
Before it fully breaks

But still
I wear a mask
Still I wear a smile
Me and suicidal thoughts
We ain't spoken in a while

I've been alone inside my mind now for days
Travelling through a contradictory maze

So answer me this...
Who's gunna free me from the troubled past
That shackles me
I'm begging
I'm pleading
Just to be set free

From this place of bitter heartbreak
This mental prison of no escape
From the darkness of past mistakes
Free from how much one person can take.

TEARS CRIED

How do I get past myself?

Do I have Anger in my DNA?
Do I sit and let Self-Doubt have its say?
Do I let my emotions get in the way?
Will there ever be a time when I'm actually okay?

I been away healing
Away searching
Putting my soul on the mend
In the process
It's true
Lost some friends

If tears were currency
I'd be a millionaire
Or in this current climate
And where I'm at
Actually, I'd be a billionaire.

So last night I said a prayer
Filled with anger
Because this shit ain't fair

Sent it out to the universe
Waiting for a response

Still waiting …

DADDY ISSUES

Daddy issues manifesting from when I was young
I've been written off
Caste off since like day one
He toyed with my feelings
Manipulated them for fun
Daddy issues got me thinking *Am I a bad son?*

Abandonment issues
Not enough tissues
To wipe away these tears
Cos he preyed on my all my fears
Thinking I wasn't good enough
For love, attention and materialistic stuff

I look at my brotherhood
Now they're older, they're grown
The questions, abandonment, the trauma, it's been sewn
Taught to hide their emotions, their anger, their tears
Within the armour of bravado that encases their fears
Battling with their place in the world
The pressure of the generational curse

Daddy issues ingrained from the day life began
He birthed one daughter, one son, then he ran
The number's 52
It's got me thinking of the rest
How long before they break

Their identities pushed to the test

Of its limitations
Never any consideration
For the lives that are affected
Never had the anaesthetic
Of *I love you* as emotional relief
Could never call him Dad as his name was always ___ .

Daddy issues has everyone fucked
Including me and my brothers
The effects of the absence
Are what we take out on our mothers
Cos they're the ones that stick around
In the background of our thoughts

Never taught emotional maturity
Growing up on the estate
Accustomed to the lifelong battle
With the pigment of our skin
Hating ourselves for feeling different
Absent fathers and the constant
Battle of what's within.

DEAR JAMAICA

Dear Jamaica, Can we talk?
I feel like we ain't spoken in ages
And even though we still haven't met I can picture you in my
head
But doing that, at times fills me with dread
You'll travel there one day is what was said
Even though if I'm honest I feel like a fraud
Years and years have passed since then
I'm starting to think maybe it's too late.
I picture my heritage
My lineage
All there on your back
You've carried them for generations
I guess I just want to say Thank you
Because if it wasn't for you I guess I wouldn't be here
Shedding these tears
Because the fear of rejection is real
The lack of identity is what I used to feel
I thought maybe you could give me some answers
I got told stories of you when I was younger
They made me smile
Occupied my thoughts for a while
Stories of newborns' umbilical cords buried beneath trees
It's said to give the baby a permanent connection with their
homeland
If so, what does that mean for me?
I mean I want a piece of that freedom

Some part of that connection
You make up so many branches in my life
From your food to your music
To my actual family relations
The ones who aren't Caucasian
If we ever met, would you accept me?
Even though my mum's white and you only make up
half of me?
If I flew to the tiny island in the sea
Would some part of my identity finally be free?
Would you love me like I was one of your children?
Because you're the motherland to many of my family tree
So surely that makes you part-motherland to me?
I guess deep down I'm just scared
Because that's not what a lot of people will see
I'm scared of what it'll actually mean for me

I really do hope we get the chance to meet one day
I mean that
Because I've got so much that I want to say
It just can't all be articulated in a letter
But when we do finally meet, it'll make me feel better
About where I fit in the world
My place among it all
Because being mixed-race has been a rollercoaster
A confusion of identity and not fitting in
You may not have all the answers
To the questions that I want to ask
But please be patient with me
Only now I'm taking off my mask

FATHER IS THE SON

Brace yourself we're going on a trip down memory lane
There's demons, there's nightmares, there's histories of pain
With all these thoughts in my head you'd think I'd go insane
Need to let them loose before they overload my brain

If I bare my soul, will I finally be free?
Delve down deep
Show you the realest side of me

I'm standing bare carrying the weight
In front of the mirror asking myself *Am I too late?*
To delve into my past, put my demons straight
Stop this cycle of self-hate -
I no longer wanna participate

Do you see a God in me?
With superpowers
Charm and charisma
Like I did my father
If so, then aren't I him?
The Father is the Son
If that's the case, then hasn't he won?

I WONDER...

...what happens when you fire bullets from your tongue
The damage they cause, can it ever be undone?

IV

MIRRORS

I've been contemplating recently
As I found myself in therapy
Coming to the realisation
It's not me against the world
It's simply Me vs Me

Men abandoning their responsibility is the cycle we're in
The effects of trauma buried deep within
The greatest pain is being human
Walking down a path
Of broken glass
Footsteps trodden in snow
Surrounded by people
Yet we're all still alone

There's shit I go through every day
There's thoughts in my head that get in the way
But only so much a heart can take
Before it shatters
Before it breaks
Clearly
Into a million pieces

I used to look in the mirror
And see Bitterness waving back
Now I see
Clearly, it's just me

REMINISCING

Am I on the right path or on the wrong road?
When I sit and reminisce, to be honest, I don't know.
Sometimes I feel at peace
Sometimes I feel so alone

In a vacuum screaming out at the world
Screaming out loud
Feeling this pressure to make people in my life proud
The ones on this earth
The ones looking down
Like Big Mike said
Heavy is the head that wears the crown
When I look back, am I standing on the shoulders of giants?
I look at me now in the mirror - Man, I'm just tired.

I reminisce
Look back to my past
To mistakes I can't fix

I reminisce
Look up to the sky
To the people that I miss

I reminisce
Blow them a kiss
Tell them I'll see them soon

Survivor's guilt it follows me
Wondering will I ever be set free
From this mental instability
Of why him and not me
Even though he's up there looking down
He can still see
This man I've grown up to be.
Maybe I've made him proud
As he's sat on the throne of a cloud
Maybe I've let him down
I'm not worthy of this crown

I know I gotta do better
Otherwise I'm shackled to my past forever.
Like my father before me, do I escape in attention and
women?
If so, what the fuck am I doing?
There's cracks staring back at me
Cracks in humanity
Cracks in society
Injustice constantly seeping through
From 72 lives lost in Grenfell to Schoolgirl Q

Am I a God? Or am I just mortal?
Wish I could travel through some portal
To another universe
Where I could converse
With those I've lost
Because grief enacts a heavy cost
On the soul and on the mind

Like a knot in my chest
But reminiscing at times, it ain't kind

Yet it's still where I find myself

W**** P********

Quite simply an absence

Of questionable looks aimed in your direction
Questionable looks at your features and complexion

Of cultural expectations
Weird opinions and judgemental observations

Of mental and physical effects of discrimination
Systemic and constitutionalised racism

Of being less likely to succeed because of your race
Social commentary about the look of your face

It's walking into a club, not having your hair groped
like you're some sort of attraction

It's people not assuming you're part of some gang or
faction

It's not being suspended from school because your hair
is a "disruption" to the class

It's not being stopped and searched because you're
wearing a mask

THIS GREAT BRITAIN

Rise and rise
From the shackles and chains
A history rooted in trauma and pain

Police pass us by and then reverse back
Constantly feeling like we're under attack
By the clothes we wear
The way we fix our hair

Never seeing the good side of us
In the papers, the media
The stereotypes paint a picture:
Black trauma

A small percentage of the population in Britain
Making up three-quarters of the faces in the prisons
We're still portrayed as the villain
Even though we live here in
This "Great" Britain

KING'S DILEMMA

Let's take a dive into the depths of my mind
The age-old story of Jekyll and Hyde

I mean I've been thinking about this deeply
So, let's talk about my history
The events in my past that have shaped me
Battles in the present that defined me

You look at me and see a smile
But I wear that smile like a mask
As I run run run so fast
From the demons that plague my past

Looking back when I was younger
I was always energetic and smart
Eyes in the mirror like
Damn, there's a work of art
Best of both worlds
I was blessed
But I must confess
That wasn't always the case

That gorilla nose and those fat lips on that face
Put a sea of thoughts in a confusing place
Father was a ghost
The Black in me, gone without a trace

So I now refrain
From ever saying his name
The more I learn about my family
The more I see
The scars that remain
I'm looking out at their history
All I see is shame and pain
Like looking through a window pane
Unresolved trauma from the past is bleeding into the
present

I see the pain hidden in their smiles
I see tribulations and trials
I see you
You see me

I see the lies in your truth
The truth in your lies
I see my first heartbreak
It was my father
He didn't even say goodbye

You see gold chains, bravado
Rage and Fury
All I see is a deep, deep insecurity
Armoured in tracksuits, money, Balenciagas
Masking the trauma of our absent fathers

I feel this insane pressure to provide for my family
The pressure is real, it's killing me
Everyone's problems on my shoulders, it's getting heavy
Weighing me down, legs weak they ain't even steady

The pressure and the feeling
It ain't leaving
Even has me at times heaving
But still I wear a mask
Still I wear a smile
Pressure's become a shadowy friend
He's been there for a while

I can no longer seem to hide
The emotional tide that flows
Behind all the smiles
I'm really hurting inside
Sometimes up
Sometimes down
Sometimes sat alone
Questioning the worthiness of this King's crown

The dilemma!

REMOVE THE KNOT

I am *not* good enough
I am *not* Black enough
I am *not* white enough
I am *not* accepted enough
I am *not* loved enough
I am *not* understood enough
I am *not* wanted enough
I am *not* worthy enough
I am *not* different enough
I am *not* strong enough
I am *not* funny enough
I am *not* interesting enough
I am *not* successful enough
I am *not* normal enough
I am *not* calm enough
I am *not* man enough

I am *not* enough

REMINISCING II

First of all, let me get some stuff off my chest
But don't think of me any less
I've got some thoughts
Going around in my head
Just been living with them
Don't know what to do with them

So I'll offload.

When I was 11 I lost my best friend and a piece of me
I knew back then I'd never be as happy as I wanted to be

I remember when those teachers
Said I'd never have a future -
Be in jail or dead
Cos even kings can lose their head
But
I've come too far
Over the past couple of years -
People's opinions
Yeah, they do just get on my nerves.
I'll probably never get the flowers I deserve.
When people judge past mistakes
The work I make
Full of hate
Like people can't change
People can't grow

Transformation
When I had a brief encounter with
Death.
Lloyd and Chloe standing in front of me
Whispering *Con, this world isn't done with you yet*

So now I'll look judgement dead in the eye
Be ok with it
Because where I am right now in my life
It won't deaden my spirit.

RIP Lloyd I know you're up there and you can see
Looking down, I hope you're proud of me
At what I've gone on to achieve
Trust me you'll never believe
That I changed it all around -
The one thing I wish is that your feet were still here
With me on the ground.

Sometimes I look back and think this life isn't fair
Especially with the cards we were dealt
Then I take a moment to stop and stare
And reminisce on the feelings that were felt.

DOMINOES

FORGIVENESS

I no longer see grey
I now, slowly,
After many years of running
See the pigment in my pain
The thoughts are still there
Whizzing around my brain
But
They're no longer making me go insane

No matter what I do
I'm not good enough for you
Not Black enough
Not white enough
But
What can I do?

See
I started the healing
After years stuck in survival mode
Facing the reality:
Forgiveness, it's a lonely road.
I'm not the same Connor
That I used to be
I took time
Was selfish
I invested in me

Unshackled the trauma of my past
Finally slowed down after running so fast
Last week I found Forgiveness
Her youthful face glancing at my file
She was stern with this gentleness
Her lips turned into a warm smile
Laid her brown eyes on my tired face
Like a parent comforting a child
And just said *Connor, where have you been?*
I've been waiting for you for a while.

I WONDER...

...if when I take my last breath
Will I finally be able to rest?

NOTES

p. 21 'Everyone falls in love sometime' is a lyric from Beenie Man's song of the same name.

p. 25 'The Branches of Me' was co-written with Jodi Ann Nicholson.

p. 32 'Grey' first appeared in *The World Reimagined: A Poetic Journey of Discovery*, edited by Adam Lowe.

p. 59 'Still Awake' first appeared in *Lucent Dreaming* issue eleven.

p. 60 The quotation from Chadwick Boseman is from his 2018 commencement speech at Howard University.

p. 67 The line 'Sometimes I think I should change my name to Why.' is inspired by *My Name is Why* by Lemn Sissay.

p. 79 The opening line is in reference to Kendrick Lamar's song *m.A.A.d city*.

p. 85 'Heavy is the head that wears the crown' is in reference to Stormzy's song *Crown*.

ACKNOWLEDGEMENTS

Where to start...

Growing up never in my wildest thoughts did I think I'd have a book. Especially one so intimate and personal as *Dominoes*.

But *Dominoes* is an accumulation of years of experiences and growth. So many people who have believed in me, supported me, showed me love. I have so many people to thank for that -

First and foremost, Lucent Dreaming. Well, most notably Jannat... Your dedication to help create something meaningful and memorable knows no bounds. Thank you for believing in my words and my stories, and believing they would resonate with others. Without you there is no *Dominoes*. Thank you for your patience, laughs, edits and gentleness as I navigated through a minefield of words and troubled thoughts, and thank you for seeing a voice in me that I didn't even see in myself.

I owe you so much. Not only did I find someone in you who championed my work and words - more than I probably did at times - but by the end I found a friend.

Gotta shoutout my mum. Wouldn't be here without you. Quite literally.

And Blade for being my brother and also my best friend. I love you both unconditionally.

Jace - Thank you for giving me the motivation to be better and to do better. Love you always Little Man.

Jodi, Mel, Lisha & Brooke - Love you and thank you for being my second family and sticking with me through those teenage times where all I saw was grey.

Love to Cynthia for being my cousin but also a sister, for being my go-to for guidance and advice. You're the realest!

Gemma and The Riverfront team! What we saying!! For always allowing space for me to talk through thoughts and feelings with you all. For guiding and supporting me on this journey that is life, and for developing a local artist and his craft through generosity and support.

Your belief in the feats I can achieve artistically is beyond anything I could wish for.

I have to give mad love to Debris Stevenson who has pushed my craft and talent to places I never thought I could go. You've opened up my mind to what I can achieve artistically, where my words and imagination could take me. I'm forever grateful to have a mentor and a friend in you. Your words have levelled me up and made me a better writer than I could have ever dreamed of.

Emma, you took a chance on me and that empowered me beyond anything in recent times in my life. You took my words and story and believed in it and in me. That's something words can never do justice. All I can say from the bottom of my heart is thank you.

Branwen, thank you for being one of the most wonderful and humble human beings I have the pleasure of having in my life. Your continued support means I go from strength to strength.

Bryony Kimmings, you QUEEN! What's there to say other than that. You've given me so much and I hope I've made you proud.

Frazer, you bossman. Without you and your wisdom I wouldn't have the confidence I have. Thank you for seeing in me talent I haven't believed was there.

And Elise - Thank you for flicking that first actor domino over ten years ago. You gave me an opportunity and with that I soared, so thank you for that. Without you there is no Connor Allen.

I am grateful to LOYALTY (Lizzie, Gabz, Jodi, Taylor, Jas, Jo-el & Jalisa) for being my artistic brothers and sisters. Always teaching me and always believing in me. You guys are the future!

And to my closest friends James, Charlotte, Katherine, Lady Elworthy, Shauna, Kim, Luke, Dave, Lucy, Oraine, Alex, Justin. Thank you all for being a part of my village and for guiding me and supporting me when I didn't have the strength within myself. Mad love!

Every interaction in my life, every person has had an effect on me in some way, big and small. I never take for granted the impact people can and have had on my life. I am who I am today because of the culmination of every person.

Lastly thanks to Book Council Wales whose support of Lucent Dreaming has made this possible.

ABOUT THE AUTHOR

Connor Allen is an award-winning multidisciplinary artist and the Children's Laureate Wales (2021-2023). He has written for BBC Wales, BBC Radio 4, Wales Millennium Centre, Sherman Theatre, Dirty Protest, and others, and is a former member of the BBC Wales Welsh Voices and The Welsh Royal Court writing groups. His work is heavily inspired by elements of his own life including grief, love, masculinity, identity and ethnicity.

An actor graduate from Trinity Saint David, he wrote and performed in his acclaimed debut show *The Making of a Monster* at the Wales Millennium Centre in 2022 (playtext published by Aurora Metro Books). He was the 2023 winner of the Imison Award at the BBC Audio Drama Awards for his debut audio drama *The Making of a Monster*. In 2021, he won the Rising Star Wales Award, and was a Jerwood Live Work Fund recipient. He is Associate Artist of his hometown theatre The Riverfront in Newport.